"You Said WHAT!?!?

The Challenges of Communicating in Life

By

William Kozlovsky

© 2003

A Search for Intelligent Yet Practical Day-to-Day Management

*"Shall I be content with lesser things and live a life of ease;
or stand with God, endure the strife and face the angry seas?"*

unknown

Copyright © 2003
William Patrick Kozlovsky

All rights reserved. No part of this book may be reproduced in any form without permission in writing from the author.

ISBN 978-1-60458-757-9

Printed in U.S. by Instantublisher.com

ACKNOWLEDGMENTS

Even a manuscript of very modest scope and size such as this could not be accomplished without the influence and assistance of many others.

I am deeply indebted to my father and to numerous associates, bosses, mentors, teachers, subordinates, peers and friends who have helped shape my own management philosophies.

Special thanks go to Ms. Melanie Schleef and Ms. Patti Kozlovsky, whose computer expertise and endless editing questions produced this text despite my writing style idiosyncrasies.

Finally, I am eternally grateful to my wife, Teri, and our five wonderful children, Susie, Bill, Patti, Janni and Kaela, who doggedly encouraged me to complete this endeavor. It is to them that I dedicate this manuscript.

TABLE OF CONTENTS

      FOREWORD

I   COMMUNICATING – WHERE THE RUBBER MEETS THE ROAD

II   GOOD IDEAS AND SANDBOXES

III   WE HAVE A PROBLEM!

IV   ISLAND OF MISFIT TOYS (OR EVERYONE HAS SOMETHING TO CONTRIBUTE)

V   PLANNING AND THE DAILY CRISIS

VI   PRODUCTIVITY

VII   HONESTY, INTEGRITY AND TRUTH

VIII THE 'WHITE PAPER'

IX   AN EXAMPLE: MANAGING A MODEST MUSEUM

X   MYSTICAL MANAGEMENT MADE SIMPLE

FOREWORD

The last several decades have seen quantum advances in technology available to management of both for-profit and non-profit entities. These advances have had major impacts on the conduct of business and the management of resources. Many of these technological improvements have significantly affected our ability to communicate more rapidly, more efficiently and more globally (in fact universally). However, it remains an enigma that, despite these advances, there has been little improvement in the human dimension of communicating and conducting business.

Casual observation across a broad spectrum of business activities reveals that human communication one to another, regardless of medium or methodology, is greatly affected by the complexity of the human being involved. A major outcome of our human involvement is the frequent disparity between what is meant (and said), and what is heard (and understood) – e.g. between what is transmitted and what is received – orally, electronically, or by the written word. The end results of this human communicating phenomenon range from trivial to catastrophic, humorous to maddening, and minor deviation from intended outcome to major misunderstanding. Witness a recent major space probe failure because of the human breakdown in communicating Metric versus English dimensions. We, the human link in the technological communication chain, remain (or are rapidly becoming) the weak link.

Many of the recurring and difficult problems that seriously affect the efficiency of organizational accomplishment and/or lead to serious personal and personnel problems in the workplace result from this phenomenon.

Acknowledging this, the purpose of this book is to address the resulting environment in a practical way for the person tasked with achieving results through the direction of human endeavor. It is intended as a philosophical look at people in the workplace, how they impact day-to-day operations and the direction of work effort toward goal achievement. The following chapters do not represent a literature search of leadership or management dictums. This book is not a "how to" or a "do-it-yourself" management book. It is not a cookbook with recipes for success nor is it a learned treatise. Hopefully, it provides some insight into successful management of modest size organizations and working level elements of large organizations given these communicating constraints.

Chapter I

Communicating – Where the Rubber Meets the Road

People get things done. Oh yes, they need tools of the trade, skills and abilities, training, education, even experience. But, bottom line results start with the prime mover – the human. Consequently organizations, businesses, agencies, and governments are all populated *at some level* with people. Except in the case of the sole proprietorship, human communication, one to another, is required in the organizational effort. Formal organizations draw up mission statements, articulate goals and objectives, set up formal or informal relationships to reach their goals, and then proceed with their day-to-day business – obtaining necessary resources (capital, labor, technology,) assigning tasks and responsibilities, introducing the human element, planning and finally (hopefully), producing the desired results. At every step some form of communication is required - within the organization and external to the organization. And, technologically no matter how it is done – face-to-face, iPhone, Blackberry, phone, fax, e-mail, web, radio, or even visual signals – it is done between and among humans. Ah – there's the rub!

How many times have we said aloud or to ourselves, "that's not what I *heard (understood)*!" – or, "gee – why didn't he/she *say* so!" – or, "boy, nobody told me," - or, "I thought you said metric", etc. Why is it that 10% never get the word?

Acknowledgment of this phenomenon is the first step to being an effective manager, whether you are a team leader, first line supervisor, department head, director, COO, President, CEO or Chairman. In order to succeed you must be able to communicate effectively. Otherwise you are doomed to an existence of frustration and an inefficient, maybe even ineffective, group/organization.

Once this is acknowledged, you can take steps to improve your communication with others and even help them improve their communication.

One technique is to start with a quick introspection – "in this situation what would *I* need/like to hear so I could respond in the way I want others to respond to me?" Essentially this is a "do unto others …" approach. It will assist you to communicate in a way to get the *intended* message across. Add to this the usual admonition to be clear, concise, brief, thoughtful, etc., and you have a good start. Be careful to remove *your* mood, emotion, and personal bias from the communication – they only clutter your message. The receiver may not be attuned to your mood, emotion, or personal bias, and therefore misinterpret your intended message. For instance, just because you skipped breakfast this morning shouldn't translate into a bad news boss, or bad messages from the boss day.

How about the ***medium***? While exogenous variables may restrict your choices, it is a good idea to consider the possibilities and their appropriateness to the message you are trying to convey. E-mail is quick and easy, but faceless. Memos and written directions are formal and documented, but evoke no body language from either sender or receiver. Video conferencing is nice when convenient, but where is the spontaneous response? Face to face is often best if you have the courage and confidence, because it permits facial expressions, body language, instant feedback, opens dialogue to clear up ambiguities, and permits buy-in by participants if they believe they have *some* opportunity for discussion. As an example, in late 1999, J.C. Penney Company, Inc., the long-standing department store chain, called a meeting of *all* managers nationwide face-to-face at their headquarters in Plano, Texas – the first such since 1927 – as a new CEO moved to restore the chain to modern competitive status. Change, in particular, dictates face-to-face communication. *Choose your medium to suit your message.*

Also, be OPEN to *feedback*. When you listen with an open mind, and not a defensive posture, you will often be able to detect when your message has not been fully or well understood. The responses or questions – or even challenges – will help you refine your message, clarify it to your intended audience, and maybe even allow you to correct or modify it before you transmit it again. It could prevent you from embarrassing yourself with a message that is easily misconstrued, and will help assure that the message generates the intended output or action.

Follow-up. Delegating is a fine trait and universally embraced as a 'good' quality for a manager. However, if you don't follow up on results of a message you have conveyed that was intended to generate action or change something, you will never know whether or not you message was really understood. Check it out – you may be surprised. In any event it is the one link in communicating that provides unadulterated feedback – see for yourself. Not only does it provide a fair assessment of your ability to communicate, it also lets you see what really happens at the other end of the daisy chain in your organization.

If you have communicated effectively, listened to the feedback, and followed-up, you will undoubtedly receive some good suggestions and new ideas. Now, what do you do about the suggestions, and good ideas someone brings up in response to your communiqués?

Chapter II

Good Ideas and Sandboxes

So, what about good ideas? Do you need them? I suspect you have learned that no one has a corner on the market of good ideas. They may come in response to your message in communicating some direction or information as noted in the prior chapter, or they may be spontaneous. They may come from peers, superiors, subordinates, or random sources. And you may *like or dislike* them (at least initially). So, what do you do with them?

First, remember there are ideas and there are IDEAS. From some people the words "I have an idea" can, and should, strike terror in your heart. I know a marketing director who had a "great idea" everyday and many of them were harebrained schemes that were impossible, impractical, not cost effective or somewhere out on the lunatic fringe. But … every so often one of these "great ideas" was brilliant – germane, within the art of the possible, exciting, productive and a quantum leap forward in what we were doing. The real challenge was to recognize the brilliant idea, pounce on it, implement it, and gently dismiss the rest.

So, you can either be a success by being a genius and having all the 'good ideas' yourself, or, you can be an average person with the genius to listen, recognize good ideas, no matter the source, when they come along and then *do* something with them. I dare say most of us must strive for the latter category. *This takes the rare ability to not be intimidated by subordinates who are smarter than you.* Surround yourself with the best people you can find and get the best ideas to get the best results.

At the same time you must also be able to turn down ideas that are not so great without offending the person offering the idea. The best way is to acknowledge the idea, but

caveat acknowledgment with an honest and gentle rejection, e.g.
- An explanation of why it can't be used, or
- "We can't use it now/here," or
- "Let me think about it," or
- "Let's see if it might be something we could possibly do."

Don't forget that some good staff ideas may be beneath your threshold of pain, but can be improvements and make a difference in either substance or process. So, don't dismiss the 'I have an idea' or 'I have a thought' too quickly. A positive alternative is to accept the idea. Tell the suggestor it is a good idea, and then empower him/her to implement it. This is a win-win, because you have not accepted a workload that you don't need or want, yet you have made a positive impact on both the operation, and on the morale of the staff member who recognized a problem and thought of a solution.

One of the difficulties with new ideas and suggestions for change or improvement is that they often impact other members of the organization directly and negatively. Why? Because very often we are all experts at suggesting how *someone else* can improve things, do things differently or do things better *in their job*.

Here enters my 'sandbox' discussion. In structured or semi-structured organizations people have formally or informally described responsibilities and hopefully commensurate authority to act. Each is a "sandbox" which is his or hers to work in, accomplish, control, be responsible for, and ultimately be accountable for. Even in unstructured free-flow organizations people invariably carve out some "turf" that is their own – a sandbox of sorts. Regardless of what is defined as your "turf" or sandbox – you will find some of your sense of self within that perimeter. It is yours to work, control, build from, accomplish, enjoy and make your mark. Your ego is a part of the equation. Naturally, you interface internally with other people who have their own sandboxes and occasionally you may even share some overlapping part of a sandbox.

You live and breathe in your work life in your sandbox. And thus, woe to the person who starts messing up, or with your sandbox. So – when someone says "I have an idea", or "why don't we …" – and it has to do with what you consider *your* sandbox, your first reaction will not necessarily be positive but more likely defensive – for several reasons. One, you are probably overworked already and someone heaping more on your plate doesn't strike a resonant cord. Two, you doubtless know more about the issue at hand than the suggestor (after all, you *live* in your sandbox) and have probably already thought of and dismissed, the idea, tried it and found it ineffective, or found that it doesn't fit philosophically with your idea of how to do your job. How to solve this dilemma?

- Discuss the idea privately with the sandbox owner before making a "public announcement" suggestion.
- Offer suggestions, or better yet "thoughts," to someone but *never* interfere with, or make commitments for them.
- Make sure your sandbox is *perfect* before you start trying to improve the next person's.
- Be sensitive to the fact that you probably don't have the full picture when you see where someone else could improve what/how they handle their responsibility.

Whatever you do, do not point out what you perceive to be someone else's shortcomings in public. It doesn't change anything, it makes the 'someone else' angry, it destroys teamwork, and it makes *you* look bad.

Success requires teamwork – people have to work together, because they depend on such teamwork for success. So, stay out of other people's *sandboxes*! Comment, communicate, coordinate, but do not interfere. We each have different personalities, styles and approaches to a task or set of tasks. Stay in your sandbox and clean up *your* mess!

Chapter III

"We Have a Problem"

This is a statement you will hear often – and the higher you rise, the more often it will come to **you**, with the expectation that you will find the solution to *our* problem.

First thing to do is LISTEN. Get a feel for the issue and whether it really is a problem or just an annoyance. If it is just an annoyance, it probably needs some attention but not necessarily yours. If you think it is a big enough annoyance for you to get involved, review the bidding. Who is in the best position to address it and try to resolve it? Do *you* need to take ownership? If not, move it to the lowest level in the organization that can, and probably should have, a try at it. If that works, good decision! If not, it will doubtless rise back up to you again and you can have another try at it by delegating – or, maybe it really is necessary for you to get involved.

What if it is a real PROBLEM? It is a good idea to remind yourself (and your staff if they are enmeshed in it) of your perspective on *problems.* What perspective? The one that categorizes problems into several levels such as these:

Level 1: epic, esoteric, probably insoluble by us at least in the near term – glacial creep, natural disasters like earthquakes, floods, blizzards, the weather, etc.
Level 2: solvable, but beyond our ability to solve at our level – war, famine, economic uncertainty, the national debt, global warming, pestilence, national policies, government pay raises, changes in state and federal tax code, etc.
Level 3: we can solve but require resources we don't control or may not have at this time – large capital improvements, local politics, public sector compensation, etc.

Level 4: these we can solve – within our control, resources, and authority – company policies, on site facilities, organizational procedures, private sector compensation, personnel practices, etc.

Don't even try to address levels 1 and 2 – it is unreasonable, except in rare cases, to expect you to do so. Level 3 is a stretch. Ask yourself – is the problem severe or important enough for you to muster the huge effort it would take in time, treasure and talent in order to acquire control of the resources necessary to take a shot at it? Maybe, if it is a serious matter of principal, survival, the "natural good," etc. But probably not. Most likely it will be good to at least consider the idea of laying some groundwork for the eventual solution of the problem, e.g. doing the *planning* necessary to start the process for approval and funding of the major capital improvement. This could be your contribution to your successor(s).

What about level 4? Here is where you *can* make a contribution – a positive impact – with the right approach. These are things within your control to influence or change. So, ask some questions:

- *Who* says it is a problem?
- Is it a problem that *needs* to be solved? Or is it just an isolated 'bitch' from someone?
- Is there an obvious solution?
- What is the benefit of solving it?
- What is the *priority* of this issue?
- Are there proposed solutions?
- Are the proposed solutions 'good ideas'? (see prior chapter re: "Sandboxes & Good Ideas")
- Who benefits?
- Who loses?
- Should others be consulted? Is it in *their* sandbox?
- What are the side effects of solving it?
- Do solutions bring other problems?
- Is there a group solution?

If your *problem* successfully passes screening using this checklist, then maybe you should just see what you could do about a solution. But – remember – there is no free lunch. Nearly all changes involve some risk of unintended downside effects appearing somewhere else in the organization or process. Often you are in a zero-sum game, and when someone or something gains, someone else/something else, loses. Also, - you can't 'make a silk purse out of sows ear' – there are trade offs and you are making them in most problem-solving situations.

So, once you have accepted a problem for solution and implemented a solution, watch carefully to see that it has the intended result and what the side effects may be. The feedback loop here is very important. Did the "we have a problem" person participate in the solution? Help or hinder a broadly acceptable solution? Were there any hidden agendas? Hopefully not. Was it really just an 'annoyance' after all?

Occasionally solving a problem can be virtually cost free. I am reminded of an occurrence when a problem of resource distribution arose among a working group of over 100 people. The problem involved a large number of conflicting "wants" for improved quality of work life, with only limited dollars available to satisfy the wants, and hence a general dissatisfaction with the lack of progress toward solutions.

The responsible manager decided to gather everyone together in one room at one time to discuss the problem. In that meeting all were asked about what was needed/wanted and it soon became apparent that there were really *two* problems. First, there was not enough money to do everything everyone wanted. Second, there was a lack of communication among the parties concerning this fact. As a result there was no attempt by the group to get together and decide *among themselves* what their priorities were. Tasked to prioritize among themselves, the group soon came up with a communal list in priority order which was very satisfactory to all – and 80% of the priority list could be funded by the dollars available. Virtually all were satisfied, because they each had *some* of *their* "wants" on that 'do-able' list. The remaining 20% of the list consisted mostly of projects that had a very low benefit/cost ratio, or had single (or few) advocates, or both. The priority list made this readily apparent, and all moved on to more productive things on the list.

In this case, tackling the 'problem' head on resulted in a win-win. Communications were improved, progress could be made, and everyone was satisfied with the outcome. They were each part of the solution and therefore bought into the outcome. What started out as a complaint and 'bitch' session, wound up as a positive constructive morale boosting planning session. The manager took time to listen, to understand the issue, and then suggest a resolution 'outside the box' with group participation. The *real problem* surfaced during the process.

It doesn't always turn out this way. But, it is worth giving it some thought. Is what I'm hearing the *real problem*? If not, how can I best uncover the real problem so we can try to find a reasonable and satisfying solution? Some digging is in order – LISTEN, QUESTION, REFLECT and ACT. This is a good sequence to follow. But stay out of the 'do loop' of trying to resolve level 1, 2, and 3 problems. If you *must* address level 3, remember to make it clear that solving the problem – maybe even any progress toward the solution – is a long term effort unlikely to show benefits or solutions to most of those involved in it now.

Chapter IV

"The Island of Misfit Toys"
or
"Everyone (Almost) Has Something to Contribute"

People! How easy it would be to manage robots and not have to deal with people and all of their problems, idiosyncrasies, moods, and intricacies, But, alas even with rampant automation, increasingly sophisticated robotics and superb technological advance, people still are part of the management equation. So, for the foreseeable future people labor will still be an economic factor of production.

This means you as a manager will *have to* deal with, work with, obtain, control, satisfy, and ultimately value them and their contribution to your effort. How best to do it?

Given your need, their importance to your productivity and the key role they will play in your success (or lack there of), it should be obvious that one of your most critical, if not *the* most crucial tasks you have, is the acquiring of people.

When you bring people to bear on your issues, no matter where they come from – internally or externally, transfers or new hires, assignments or volunteers – you *must* give it your very best effort because managing your workforce is the ultimate factor in your success. *I can't emphasize too strongly the importance of the acquiring process.*

Why? You only get one real chance to immediately influence the character of your workforce – and it is here. Anything after hiring is minor tuning. Be it sports, performing arts or business – the team and its ultimate abilities is shaped by its people.

So, don't be rushed, bullied, or casual in your selection of people for your team. Better a few days, weeks, or even months short handed than years handicapped because of a poor hiring decision.

If you have the choice to select *your entire* group (team, staff, etc.), you are in 'Fat City'. Your fate is in *your* hands in the hiring process. But few of us have that luxury. Usually you inherit at least a major portion of the group. So, acknowledging the importance of hiring new, additional or replacement people (you have vowed to do that right) – how about the hand you've been dealt in this situation? Well, as the old saying goes you will have to "grin and bear it" in the beginning.

Best thing to do at this point is take stock of what you have been blessed (cursed) with. The "ignorance is bliss" idea may have some merit, but your bliss will be short lived if you are not conscious of the characteristics of the team you have inherited. Thus you should use your skills and your own style to find out about each member. Some managers like to interview, others like to observe, and many like to probe, challenge, and then evaluate. No one way is best and no one way gives perfect results – a full picture of each person's capabilities, strengths, weaknesses, prejudices, styles, stimuli, etc. But you need to give it your best try in order to prepare yourself for the learning process you are entering, and for your survival during the first few days, weeks, and months of your new endeavor.

It is not enough to do this with your own team if you are entering a new company, group, division, project, etc. There you must also evaluate your environment – particularly your peers. You don't get to 'hire' them, but they can be just as important to your success as your own team, and much more devious. Don't forget them, find out as much as you can about them.

What to look for? At this point you may feel like you have stumbled across Santa's "Island of Misfit Toys" – the toy train with square wheels, the spotted zebra or the striped lion, the 'Jill in the box,' etc. Don't despair yet. Here are some examples of what to look for besides the normal, hard-working, reasonable people like most (?) of us. Be on the lookout for: Chatty Kathy, Time Waster, Crisis Mistress, Know It All,

Promoter, Mr. "I have a good idea," "We need to talk," "I need to bring you up to date," 'I hurt my back" slacker, Gold Brick, Mr. Clipboard, Ms 'Poor Me,' Complainer, Undercutter, Powerbroker, Mr./Mrs. "wear the bosses position," the "drunk but indispensable," Mr./Mrs. "did you know…," Clock-watcher, 'Bosses Favorite,' Mrs. Passive, the Bully, 'Yes'-person, 'No'-person, Fault-finder, and many more.

Hopefully, you will not have any – or at least just a few folks with some of these characteristics who impinge upon you and your efforts. But if you *do,* you need to add that ingredient into your management thinking. Each requires a different approach, response and level of oversight. Forewarned is forearmed. Ignoring your misfits can be hazardous to your management, and career, and health. There are numerous good seminars and short courses that train managers how to deal with these types and you can learn techniques from them on how to deal with difficult people of all sorts.

Sounds like doom and gloom, but usually there is a silver lining in the cloud somewhere (a pony in that pile of…). *"Everyone (almost) has something to offer."* Try to adopt the philosophy that your challenge is to find what that "…something to offer" is, and then figure out how to apply it to the advantage of your project or effort. When you accept this challenge, your overall frustration level with people will decrease considerably over time and your team effort will be much more productive. Admittedly this can be easier said than done.

This is a more creative – and perhaps more positive – approach to take in handling people because, rather than deal with their negativity, it recognizes the positive potential they have and concentrates on dealing with that potential. I like this philosophy because it concentrates on making lemonade out of lemons – adding the sugar if you will – and has the side effect of bringing out the best in people because you play to and utilize their strengths. Rather than constantly counter play (ping-pong) their negative aspect, you relegate it to the back burner by utilizing the good they are able to bring to the table.

And sometimes it actually ameliorates or even changes the 'bad' behavior and brings out the best in the individual.

Does it work? – Yes, usually. Is it easy? – No. But, it is usually as easy or easier than the battle of wits that you would otherwise engage in, and it can be a real satisfying experience to bring out the best in someone. It does require both insight and flexibility (creativity) to properly utilize what they have to offer in the context of your organization and your objectives. Try it! You might like it. There is a place for almost everyone if you are creative enough to find what it is and put them in that place. You may have to think outside the box, but that is one of the marks of a superior manager of people. Indeed it is possible to productively place the "misfit toys" as long as you remember "almost everyone has something [good] to contribute".

Chapter V

Planning and the Daily Crisis
or
'Life is What Happens While You're Making Plans!'

We need plans – and planners. Plans help us articulate our goals and objectives and lay out the road map for reaching them. They help us structure our trip along the path we want to travel.

Do plans guarantee a successful journey? Certainly not. But without them – formal or informal – you can almost guarantee an *un*successful journey. If you don't know where you're going, any road will take you there – and that "there" most likely will not be where you really wanted to go.

Why doesn't good planning guarantee a successful journey? Because "life is what happens while you're *making* plans." Ah, yes – the daily crisis. The unexpected. The sudden changes in our environment. These are the detours, the roadblocks, the potholes of management travel along the highway of plans and their execution. Sometimes it is just the Monday morning syndrome – nothing seems to go right. Or it is the unexpected phone call that requires an immediate action or response. Sometimes it is sickness, the weather, a family crisis, the car won't start, something is lost and can't be found, the traffic, the airport, - the unexpected, and therefore unplanned. Occasionally it is our fault. We lost something, forgot something, or didn't follow our plan. But usually it is an exogenous variable – some thing beyond our control visited on our plans and us by *someone* else, e.g. Mother Nature, a staff member, family, a customer, etc. It could also be *some*th*ing* – failed gizmo, faulty gadget, etc. which demands our immediate action, interaction or response – or has an impact on our plan and us. In any event it is a factor we had not anticipated and had not included in our plan.

So, what do we do now? In football it means we drop back and punt – hoping to get another chance to put our plans into action. Or we can cry a lot and hope the problem goes away. We can get angry and try a forced play – drive on with the plan for the day despite the problem (like going to work in a snowstorm). Some will recognize the need for a slight detour and adapt to it.

But in any case it is necessary to adjust. Your challenge is to: (1) recognize the interruption (2) determine if it necessitates an adjustment to your plan(s) (3) estimate the magnitude of the impact and then (4) decide what to do about it. What you *don't* want to do is ignore it, hoping it will go away. There are even times when it is best to give up (I'm sure you've felt this one), realize it is just "one of those days," hold your plan(s) in abeyance for the time being, and shift to crisis reaction mode for the day with the resignation that comes from experience knowing that this day is "just not going to go as I had planned." When you come to this conclusion it allows you to devote your full time and energy to resolving the crisis or crises that seem predestined to come to you this day and then, hopefully, get back on track with your plan tomorrow. As Annie sings in the fabulous Broadway play – "tomorrow, tomorrow, I love you tomorrow, you're only a day away."

This brings us to flexibility. Some people are able to survive nicely in the world by using "go with the flow" philosophy. It eliminates most of their frustration in life and allows them to adapt to most any situation. But many (most?) of us want to *control* the flow, not go with it. Can it be done? Yes. – Always? Probably not. – Why not? Look at it terms of scale. If you are able-bodied you can probably control the flow of water in a small creek with just a shovel to change or direct its path. Not so with a stream or river. There you would need a bigger, more powerful tool. Even then in a raging storm you probably will lose control. So it depends on *you* and the size and scope of the *tools* you have to control your environment. The secret to success here is knowing what is within your power to control, what is beyond your power to control and acting accordingly. A couple of clichés come to mind. Don't fall on your sword over a trivial matter. Don't use the windward side if you are seasick. Pick your fight wisely. Don't take on a wild beast you can't kill because if you just wound it, you will just make it mad and you will be a big loser.

There are warning signs of some pseudo crises. Recognizing them can help eliminate the constant interruption of your carefully laid plans for progress. One of these is the "hall job." You are proceeding apace – en route to some rendezvous – making progress on your days plan – when someone encounters you in the hall who "needs a little help" or "need you to decide." *Never* allow yourself to be trapped by this person. Unless you promptly (but politely) move them back into a regular process you will wind up making a hasty judgment or decision without full knowledge of the facts and have *your* day's agenda inconveniently interrupted to suit their schedule and agenda. Usually a bad deal all around for you – a poor decision, which will probably have to be revisited, an interruption of your plan and time lost. How then to deal with the situation. One way is to recognize the importance of the person and their issue ("That sounds like a problem we need to get to promptly."), and then set a schedule for discussion at a *mutually* convenient time ("Why don't we get together about 11 o'clock and work through it?" – or "I am on a mission right now but I'll stop in on my way back – 30-40 minutes and you can bring me up to date.") Now you are back in control of your life. Of course, if the issue is a bonafide emergency, it isn't a hall job but a real crisis and *does* need to interrupt your day for immediate attention.

Another productivity killer is the dreaded meeting – 'staff,' 'group,' 'special,' 'project,' etc. We will deal with that in 'Museum Operations.'

Next comes e-mail. Why is it that people think they can palm responsibility and workload off on you just by sending you an e-mail, when they know they could not do so be telephoning or meeting with you? Don't fall into this trap. Don't let others pass their workload 'monkey' to you by sending you directive or response requiring e-mail, voice mail or text, unless they happen to be your boss. Likewise don't pass your workload 'monkey' to others. Often e-mail is the adult equivalent of the two-year-old technique of whining – it persists until it gets you to do something. As a manager I tell others I don't respond to e-mail. I will read it on *my* schedule, but not react to it, especially if it tries to task me. If you want to task me you'd better call or meet so we can *discuss* the issue, reasons for passing a workload to me and the parameters of my response. Don't be regulated by a need to act on e-mail. How often do you act on a telephone message left for you by a peer or subordinate directing you to take action or workload? Rarely, I suspect, without discussing the matter personally in some detail. E-mail, voice mail or texting is only slightly better. Ignore it when you wish, answer it when you get around to it, act on it only if it is in your self-interest. Otherwise you'd be surprised how many 'bosses' you will have!

Ditto for voice mail. Generally the protocols that grew up with voice mail make it less likely to be a monkey passer than an information passer. But the blinking red light on the phone can be a seductive siren to lure you away from a planned productive process just to satisfy your curiosity. 'Maybe it's something important.' (Isn't your planned project important? If not you shouldn't have planned it!) Perhaps it is that important call-back I have been waiting for (will a few minutes longer make any difference? After all you've waited this long and it won't evaporate just because you don't listen to it ASAP!) Yes, phone tag can be annoying, but it is less burdensome than being tasked remotely by some spurious e-mail, voice-mail or text message where you are tagged and now must assume some added workload without the courtesy of a "but, sir …" opportunity for discussion.

Chapter VI

Productivity

A former boss once told me his secret to success via high productivity. "Load everyone to 200% of their capacity. They can't do that much, but they will deliver 150% while they try." That philosophy speaks to load and quantity. But, what about effectiveness?

Effectiveness has at least two components: quality and priority. I don't address quality, it has been beaten to death in all the popular and academic literature in the past decade, so you are well aware of its importance and can easily educate yourself on it. What about priority?

The watchword here is to be sure that not only do you do things right (quality) but that you *do the right things* (priority)! Doing the *right things* brings progress. Doing things right but not paying attention to what are the *right things* results in dithering – activity and effort but no progress – busy work but not necessarily business.

Doing the *right thing* is no easy job. Someone (read you) must assure that the tasks undertaken are important to, and will result in progress toward, your *major* goals and objectives. If you are not eternally vigilant there are many distractions to keep you from your priorities!

First is the "in-box" syndrome. Doing things right means taking care of the "in-box" – be it e-mail box, correspondence in-box, or telephone answering. It is 'oh so easy' to fall victim to dealing with all these just because they are there! They beckon to you – the stack of mail, the blinker on the phone telling you that there are messages recorded, the "you have mail" voice from your computer. They arouse our curiosity. – What's in there? Who called? And the temptation is to check it out. But, is it a convenient subconscious excuse for not working on your highest priority? Moving papers, reading e-mail, and listening to phone messages or reading email on your mobile phone is usually easier than solving tough problems or acknowledging major issues – and it gives the illusion of progress – something getting done. Solution? Can be as simple as setting certain times aside each day for these activities or as complex as a conscious effort to work them in between higher priorities as "fillers".

Next comes the "hall-job". We discussed that in the previous chapter and it definitely affects productivity.

Then there is the "ringing phone." Nothing is more discourteous to someone who has come to see you with a priority than to have you answer a ringing phone of some kind – unless it's answering a ringing phone from someone else in your organization who didn't make the effort to come personally and having *you* give that person *priority*. Unless you have prefaced your meeting with "I'm expecting a call while we're meeting," this behavior is plain rude. Voice mail will document the caller for your review later, and if it's an emergency they will find you (or solve the problem themselves). So, the advice is – DON'T.

Next on our list of distractions is the "monkey giver." This person has a workload he/she would love to get *you* to take over. An appeal to your ego, a request for a favor, use of the royal "we" will be employed, or some other genius (or devious) device to shift the monkey from his/her back to yours. This is a particularly common device employed by subordinates because they know you have the ultimate responsibility anyway – so why not get you to take over the workload. DON'T. Ask this simple question. "Have you done the very best you can do with (this issue)?" If the answer is frustrated (and humble) 'yes', it may be time for you to listen. If it isn't – then pass the monkey back with the exhortation "do the very best you can do here, and if that just doesn't work, then come see me and we will talk about it." Exit stage left.

Finally, there's the *boss*. He/she comes in with his/her latest hot idea for such and such and it should be done (acknowledged), looked at, worked on, solved, etc. (Usually ASAP is implied.) Ah – this one is more difficult. The choice seems to boil down to:

- Say "no" (and risk career self-destruction)
- Say "OK" (and reprioritize everything else)
- Say "OK" (and slide it into the priorities where it fits)
- Say "I'll look into it" (and do look into it *before* fitting it into the priority list of *right things* to be doing" – if it doesn't fit, go back for a review with the boss)

Always remember the fable of the tortoise and the hare. Who was working on the *right thing*? To win the race (be productive) it is absolutely essential to know your priorities and stick to them over the long haul.

Chapter VII

Honesty, Integrity, and Truth

Yes – do – must – for any good and self-respecting manager. On the practical side the nice thing about telling the truth is that you don't have to remember what you said. No lies, no deceit, no problems. On the ethical side it's the right thing to do, and on the business side it marks you as a person who can be trusted. A good reputation is hard to earn, easy to lose and absolutely priceless. Value yours and that of others. Look for it in others and when you find it, treasure it.

Don't confuse good news or bad news with truth. If you get good news and it's not true you may feel good for a short period but are in for a big fall when the truth becomes known (and it always does, eventually). If you get bad news and it's true, you will be unhappy, but you will know the facts and can deal with the issue without a gut-wrenching surprise down the road. You may be unhappy at the bad news, but should never "shoot the messenger." The messenger didn't create the bad news just to aggravate you. Unless you know the bad news (truth), you can't deal with it in a timely manner. And problems seldom get better with age. In fact, usually they get worse. Often a problem begins as a small annoyance that is within your capability to fix. Ignored, it grows and grows like Jack's beanstalk and, may grow too big for you to fix. Like the wastebasket fire – put it out now before it becomes a building fire or an inferno. TRUTH – real facts, even bad news - empowers you to act. Insist on it in others and never waiver from it yourself. It means you must always be HONEST – never to steal, cheat, or lie, and it marks you as a manager with INTEGRITY – having the quality of being honest and trustworthy.

The principles are easy; it is the practice that's hard. Often the same situation generates different emotions (and temptations from the truth) dependent on where *we* are in the scenario – like the old saying: "where you stand depends on where you sit …". Explaining bad news to your boss might bring a greater temptation to do a soft sell – gloss over some of the pertinent facts, shade the truth just a "little" to protect the guilty or innocent (you?), sugarcoat it just a little to ease the pain (yours?) – than explaining the bad news to subordinates. You know the boss doesn't like bad news. Bad news reflects badly on you if it was your error. So, just slide it through? Great idea, but extremely shortsighted. DON'T DO IT. Be honest, up front and factual. Take the edge off of the situation by explaining what corrective actions you are taking, not by shading the truth. You maintain your self-respect and enhance your trustworthy reputation. Our world is not painless or trouble free. Very few people are perfect. Admit it and deal with it honestly. If you have a boss who can't handle that approach, you need a new boss!

Likewise protect your boss by being honest. If the "emperor has no clothes on …", then tell the emperor that he/she is going down a road you think is dangerous, wrong, or non-productive. If he/she chooses to continue that course of action despite your warning, that choice is theirs. But you have fulfilled one of your duties as an employee by advising the boss of your perception. [Too bad no one warned Bill Clinton early on in the Lewinsky affair.] If things turn out badly, you have the self-satisfaction of knowing you did your best to warn and protect your boss (<u>never</u> "I told you so"). If it turns out you were wrong, no harm done! You just have to eat a little crow.

I digress for a moment. One of your greatest enemies in the arena of truth, integrity, and honesty is hubris – the feeling that because you have power, position, wealth, or prestige, the normal rules don't apply to you. It brings a false sense of invulnerability – the pride that goes before the fall. Hubris causes people to do things that others couldn't do without serious repercussions. They believe they are above the law and need not conform to normal rules of society. A huge ego pervades their thinking, and they become "me" centered.

The higher you get in the management chain the easier it is to get seduced by hubris. After all, who would dare challenge the boss? Who would dare tell him/her that they were 'going out without any clothes on'?

As a manager and as a decent human being, you must carefully guard against hubris. Not only is it wrong, but it can get you into a lot of trouble. What a great hubris Richard Nixon must have had to tape all his private conversations for posterity, even those conversations that clearly implicate him in the dirty tricks. But after all, he was king! He could do as he pleased with impunity.

A management consultant giving a presentation on ethics to a group of very senior government officials some years ago made an interesting point in this regard. He said "Remember that the higher the monkey climbs in the tree, the more his (bare) rear-end shows…." Don't forget that point as you climb higher in the management tree.

Integrity, honesty, and truth compel some additional attitudes. One of these is the need to look after the people you have who work under your management. They deserve your fair, honest, and full support. Not only is it your responsibility to provide them with the necessary tools to do the job – resources including money, time, people, skills, and rewards – but also to look after their human needs. Remember Maslov and his "Hierarchy of Needs." As a manager you must do your part to satisfy those needs – even if it makes you unpopular with upper management. We are all familiar with the climber who claws his/her way to the top over the backs of others. Too often it is successful, but at what price? If you are not convinced of the moral need to look after your people, look at the very selfish side. Those whom you manage will likely have the ability at some time or another to either help you or do your career harm. Life is full of quid pro quo – both good and bad. If you have supported your people in their needs, chances are they will return the favor. Likewise if you have not supported them, chances are they will return that 'favor' also. Remember that the "little guy" in the world of management (unlike the world of dictatorship) is also in a position to affect your success. In fact he/she might turn out to be *your boss* some day! Remember – *everyone* has something to offer.

Following right behind management truth and in line with integrity and honesty with people is the issue of forthrightness – being frank, open, direct, and not hinting around. For many of us this is the "64 million dollar question." Perhaps some examples are in order.

Here is a doctor's report to the patient in his office who has had a large limp in her groin for 3-6 weeks, "All of the tests I've done thus far are negative, so it must be cancer, and we'd better do a biopsy. I'm going to send you to a cancer expert."

Certainly the doctor told it like it was – from his perspective. He was frank, open, and direct. But was it best for the situation? Probably not. And good bedside manner it wasn't. The impact in this actual case was devastating to the twenties something patient. As you could imagine it conjured up terrible thoughts about the big 'C', especially since it was in the groin area and she knew that lymphatic cancer was one of the worst. For the three weeks while she waited to get to see the specialist, waiting to get the test scheduled, waited to get the results, she went through hell on earth for no good reason. The tests were all negative and the specialist concluded the swelling was most probably caused by a bite from a brown recluse spider on a camping trip several weeks before. (My advice to the patient was to get a new regular doctor – pronto!)

Is there another way to get the same message across without the 2x4 to the side of the head? I think so. How about this: "Nothing has shown up in our tests thus far so I'm going to explore some remote possibilities with some additional tests." But was it frank? Maybe. Open? Yes. Direct? Probably not – not to the extent of bluntness at least.

Was it truthful? Yes. Was it honest? Yes. Did it show integrity? Yes. And, it didn't scare the wits out of the patient. Did it "tell it like it is?" Yes. There was no deceit, no hinting, and no cover-up – just the honest admission that so far no results and *no guesses*.

Bottom line for me is: tell it like it is, but when you do so be sensitive to the recipient – have some bedside manner and don't be a bull in a china shop. There is no need to tell it with an "in your face" attitude!

Then why tell it like it is at all? Why not go with the flow, be wishy-washy and not rock the boat? Is there any good reason or redeeming social grace in being frank, open, direct, and not hinting at the issue? I believe there is - but with some qualifiers. Being open, frank and direct is efficient. You don't waste time 'beating around the bush,' hinting at the issue, hoping the message will gradually sink in. You don't have to carefully develop a story line that leads up to the situation. On the other hand, in being indirect and circumspect, you risk failure to get the *intended* message across – and all the other consequences of poor communications. Even if you get the idea across, it is difficult to assure that you have communicated the entire or correct message. Likely you will not get the same direct response and body language telling you that what you said and intended has been heard and understood, that you will by being open, frank, and direct. Then, your management world becomes a little squishy – more uncertainty if you are not open, frank, and direct.

Open, frank, and direct telling it like it is has some secondary benefits. People always know where you stand. They don't have to guess or pussyfoot around trying to find out. This generally is a good thing. People may not agree with you but they can count on knowing what you want and where you stand. There is a comfort level in certainty. The saying "what you see is what you get" is applicable here. No hidden agenda and no 'wishy-washy'. You know where you stand and can therefore proceed to do what you have to do. No ambiguity, no guessing game, no 'I wonder' – just follow the yellow brick road. Productivity increases as false starts decrease. No unnecessary running down rat holes because you aren't sure what the boss really wants or what the real situation is. So you can do your staff a big favor when you "tell it like it is."

How about the downside? The primary downside is the unintended impact as noted above with the doctor's report. If you are going to tell it like it is then be certain you *know* what it *is*. Use some tact, diplomacy, and bedside manner if the *issue* is sensitive, frightening, or ego damaging. Next – analyze your 'audience.' Be reasonably certain they/he/she are able to handle the frank, open, and direct approach. There is dangerous ground here. What to your staff or employees might be good, clear, straightforward guidance, may seem to your boss like a challenge to his authority, or to his ego, or to his security. All this is bad for you. What may seem like great communication internally might be viewed as politically incorrect externally. Challenging the ideas of your peers and/or staff in a good rousing discussion might be invigorating and eye-opening to them but may be seen as impertinent or insubordination in a group meeting with your boss. Don't forget that while the boss may not *always* be right, she/he is always the *boss*. Fools go where angels fear to tread. If your superior is comfortable with who and what he or she is, then he/she will not feel threatened by such an approach. But if he or she has been promoted to his or her level of incompetence, telling it like it is threatens their position and doing so will put you in deep *kimchi*. Bottom-line – don't unnecessarily commit career suicide by being *too* direct, frank, and open with your superiors. Unless it's a matter of *principle*, *ethics*, or *integrity*, it's probably not worth the price you will ultimately pay.

Chapter VIII

The "White" Paper

Sometimes when we look to upper management, the board of directors, or board of trustees we perceive an obstacle to what we consider progress. Many of us vowed in earlier years that if we ever reached that exalted position we would remember what it's like down below and change things, e.g. be more understanding, open to new ideas, flexible, more responsive, decisive, etc. Some of us even made notes in a diary of sorts to catalog behaviors we would avoid (or emulate) should the opportunity present itself.

Perceived or real, for better or for worse, this situation often presents itself to the middle manager, project manager, or team leader. There is a decision that needs to be made, resources need to be committed, approvals are required, or a reaction expressed. But time passes without the necessary response. Meetings are scheduled but the indecision persists – others need to be consulted, but there is no time now, etc., ad infinitum.

If you never encounter this problem, count yourself blessed. But if and when you do, consider it 'normal.' Especially if the decision involved is controversial, unpleasant, involves significant change in 'the way we do things,' or means facing up to some issues higher management would like to see just go away. If it requires a group decision, it is even worse. Group decisions are never easy. So, if it is a board or team decision you want, it will take time. Groups often look for consensus – middle ground, face saving solutions, low risk compromises. But, you need guidance/decisions *now*. So, what to do?

One approach is to prepare a decision memo. Issue, problem, cause, solution, approval. Short, sweet, simple, direct, and fast. It gets rid of the clutter, lays it on the table and says, "sign here so we can get moving." OK? If you have a boss or board that delegates well, stays out of the operating 'weeds', sticks to broad policy, appreciates the direct no frills approach to problem solving, and trusts you, then you're all set. But what if you don't? Then the plot thickens.

An effective approach in these circumstances may be the **'White Paper.'** It is longer and more difficult to prepare than a decision memo. It requires you to articulate all the things that you think are readily apparent to anyone and could be assumed, but in doing so it presents a complete picture that *anyone* can read, understand, and make decisions concerning.

The version of White Paper I like is the progressive model consisting of the following elements:

- Problem statement
- Question(s) to be answered
- Discussion
- Spectrum of alternatives available
- Pros and cons of each alternative
- Recommended alternative for implementation

The advantage of the White Paper is that it shows the reader you understand the problem, have considered the alternatives, have carefully thought through the pros and cons of each alternative, and have thus rationally reached a recommended course of action. By using the full spectrum of possibilities from Genghis Kahn to Karl Marx or Ronald Reagan to Bill Clinton, you quickly make the case for reasonableness of your position, (unless you are recommending a far right or far left solution, of course) you have narrowed the choices to the reasonable and viable solutions, with your recommendation being among them. Now you make the persuasive argument for your reasonable, well-supported conclusion. And there you have it! Well, almost….

There is some risk here. Remember the old saying "… be careful what you ask for, you might get it …"? Well, in the case of the White Paper … be careful what alternatives you give, they might pick one *other* than your recommended alternative. This means, you must be absolutely certain of your "pros and cons" so if *any* alternative is selected you can execute it. You probably don't want to go back and say 'gee, boss, we can't really do that because… or 'I forgot to mention that…' (fill in the blank)." You might even want to group your alternatives into two categories like feasible and not feasible, affordable and not affordable, practical and not practical, viable and not viable, etc. just to protect yourself. Another reason to have your pros and cons list complete and accurate is that you guard against short memories, and surprised reactions at such things as cost, or timing that accompany the selected alternative when you begin to execute. You can always point to your White Paper and remind everyone that this was part of the advantage or disadvantage of making this particular choice. In other words you have protected your flanks.

Chapter IX

An Example: Managing a Modest Museum

When it comes to the need for intelligent and practical management, small to medium sized museums come near the top of my list. Generally cash poor, non-profit and short-staffed, these museums are a great place for contributing to the community and use a wide range of managerial skills to meet the many challenges. They are a microcosm of the business world, and, if you can afford the luxury of long hours and modest renumeration, the experience can be enlightening, rewarding and a great learning opportunity.

The range of issues can be overwhelming – but they encompass every aspect you can expect to encounter in a fast track career. You will be multi-tasked, multi-disciplined, and have the opportunity to learn a little bit (usually the most critical or important "little bit") about every aspect of management – planning, policy, forecasting, budgeting, financial management, fundraising, accounting, administration, human resources, personnel, contracts, legal issues, wage and hour laws, medical plans, job descriptions, marketing, public and community relations, managing/working with volunteers, facilities maintenance and repairs, library operations, asset management, sales, merchandising, retailing, education, graphic design, - well, you get the picture.

So, why do it? Because if you spend a few years in this environment you will come face to face with enough issues, challenges, problems, and opportunities to make you a "utility infielder" in ANY job or management situation with enough broad experience to allow you to be credible and confident that your decisions will be better than most.

Let's start from the beginning – planning and building a new museum. Where to start?

First, as with any new endeavor there are many places to turn for advice. Fortunately in the museum business, particularly if you are going to be in the "small" or "medium" categories (generally, a budget under $5 million) and therefore pose no threat of serious competition to the "big" folks, there is some sense of noble purpose that seems to engender support from, and among, contemporaries. So ask – and ye shall receive – lots of good solid advice from the museum community. Learning from others' experiences is a good way to come up to speed quickly and help avoid pitfalls others have experienced. The American Association of Museums is a treasure house of good information in almost every area of museum management and operation. Membership is easy and the fee is scaled to size.

Second, apply common sense and reason to everything you do – those things discussed earlier in this book will all come in handy as a point of reference or comparison.

Third, consider some basic concept ideas and tailor then to your situation. For example, consider the following thoughts as you begin the planning:

- Remember to plan twice, but build (or renovate or organize) only once. Re-planning is easy; rebuilding is very costly.
- Avoid the common, enthusiasm driven, "FIELD of DREAMS" syndrome – "if we build it, they will come." Not necessarily so.
- Define your intended audience: who are you trying to reach, and who will your visitors/customers be?
- Clearly define your purpose regarding this audience: Educate? Entertain? Share information? Excite? Motivate? Challenge? What is our mission?
- Define, articulate and UNDERSTAND your expectations, e.g. number of visitors per day; revenue stream; public recognition.

A helpful method to come to grips with these questions is to form both a hard-core advisory (working) group of prime movers for this project, and then an AD HOC external review group to give all of your answers a "reality" check. Many will recommend a professional consulting group to help at this stage. I do not. They can lead you through the process (makes it easy, but then why pay you?) but have no long-term responsibility for OUTCOME. Your peers have lived through the process and will still be around long after the consultants have gone. Now some practical (even nitty-gritty) factors to consider:

- ❖ If you really want visitors from beyond the boundaries of your local community, seriously consider putting yourself in or at a tourist DESTINATION, as opposed to an obscure location or just a "rest stop" along the way. There is synergy (and yes, competition) in a bonafide "destination." Market research can be a big help here, and good examples abound – San Francisco, Washington D.C. (the mall), Baltimore (inner harbor) etc. LOCATION, LOCATION, LOCATION. It's not the only answer, but it can be a good or even the best answer.

- ❖ For the construction or renovation process you will need professional help. The board of trustees is a good place to find recommendations for expertise for the design and contracting phases. Doubtless they will have a committee to provide the oversight and you will merely be one player in the process. But - once the process goes to contract you will suddenly find yourself on the hot seat for making it happen. Two bits of advice:

    1. First, early in the contracting phase, insist on provisions for hiring a construction management company (or person) to be your eyes and ears for the project. They are professionals who know the

business, talk the talk, can judge performance against contract, do your quality control and keep the contractor (and his subs) honest in fulfilling their obligation under the contract. They can also screen requests for change orders for need/applicability, and can interpret for you the numerous questions/problems that will occur during the construction phase. You will have lots of other things on your plate to deal with. So unless (or maybe even if) you are a professional civil engineer, a construction management company can prove invaluable in avoiding costly overruns during construction.

2. Second, get to know the general contractor's on-site construction superintendent and establish a good, open, honest and frank relationship with him/her. This is the pressure point for immediate resolution of problems on-site – and you will be the point person to resolve safety (your staff), security (your valuables), and interference (your customers/business) problems on a day-to-day basis. Have a phone number, a pager, a cell phone number or whatever it takes to reach him/her or the contractor 24 hours a day, seven days a week.

Once underway, keep your eye on costs verses budget and schedule. Time is money. Unless there is a major surprise (e.g. you find human remains as you dig!), there is no reason to run late or over budget. Be *very tough* on change orders – allow these *only* if there is a bonafide reason that it must be done to prevent a work stoppage or to correct a major error by architect or engineer. Most "improvements" are far more costly as change orders than as later on modifications after the project is completed to spec. The contractor makes up for his shortfall in the bidding process by using change orders to get added work at premium rates. Draw the line – "NO CHANGE ORDERS," and then go from there only when you must do so to correct an error or deficiency.

OK – the job is done, the furnishings have arrived and you are ready for the hoopla of a grand opening, big public relations splash, etc.! Congratulations! You've passed the first major hurdle.

The Board

Composition of your board depends to a certain extent on the bylaws of the organization and the history you inherit. But at some point you will have an opinion about board membership and may have some input regarding changes. The four things that come quickly to mind when considering board memberships are: oversight; stature; financial support; and help.

In most cases, particularly if the museum is exempt from federal income tax, the board has a responsibility to see that the organization is operated legally and soundly – that it follows good management practices, exercises care with donated funds and in general operates in accordance with its charter and bylaws. Individually and collectively the board has a fiduciary responsibility to see that the museum is well run. The regularly scheduled board meetings, a reasonable number of specific committees (nominating, finance, audit, marketing, collections etc.) and management reports to the board carry out this oversight function. Caution: the board has an oversight and policy function– not an operations function. More than one museum has lost its way when the board or individual board members began to dictate or dabble in day-to-day operations. Operations and operating decisions are YOUR responsibility. Take care not to let board members play in your sandbox (tactfully).

As with any board of trustees (or directors) the museum board should reflect the stature of the museum in the community and in its field. Some will argue that stature is the only requirement for board membership – get big names on the letterhead and all will be well. Doors will be opened, funds will be contributed, grants will be received and all will be well. Others will argue that this approach may work occasionally – especially for large one-time fundraising campaigns, but that for the long run, more is required. In this case stature must include a genuine interest in the museum, enthusiasm for what it represents and provides to the community, and a willingness to actively participate in its oversight. Are these disparate views? Perhaps, but not necessarily. A mix of both kinds of "stature" trustees in likely to be optimal. Some (few) 'names' for ego appeal and letterhead stature 'announcing' to the world, and some (more) community names who are personally active, interested and supportive.

Then there are those board members who really want to be part of the museum, see it succeed and have the where-with all and willingness to provide continuing financial support themselves. Some of these might overlap the 'stature' category and some might not. Numerous tales abound of the trustee/director who was not a 'name' in the community but was a successful person with a genuine interest in the museum who quietly stepped up to the plate in some major funding need and quite unexpectedly assumes a major donor role. This is probably the most difficult kind of trustee to find. Much effort and investigation are required before you and your board select a person from this category for your board.

Finally there are those you need who cannot provide you with stature, a name draw, or major contribution support. But they have some expertise that a museum needs, or some connections to things your museum needs on a regular or occasional basis and you don't want to (or cannot afford to) pay for those services. For example, a good high level, articulate and knowledgeable CPA for your finance committee. An attorney willing to donate his time, pro bono, to be counsel to the museum in its many legal needs. A PR, advertising or marketing guru to work with the staff and marketing committee and/or donate advertising space and work. For a nautical museum needing occasional tug assistance; a harbor pilot, tug company owner, port captain, etc. The list goes on, but you get the idea. Hands on help with providing necessary goods and services by people with a genuine interest in the museum. It can't be beat. All will not necessarily agree, but it is worthy of thoughtful consideration as you populate or re-populate the board.

One final thought. Have your Chairman interview each prospective member over breakfast or lunch with you in attendance if possible. Then ask your Chairman if it would be possible to have the candidate meet informally with one or two other trustees to get a good feel for the fit. Fit is as important as function for a smooth running and happy board. And one of your major goals is a smooth running and happy board of trustees.

Board Meetings

Now you have your board. What next? Usually all of your board members are very busy people whose involvement with the museum is a minor item on their agenda. If they are typical, they may be able to spend an hour or two to attend a quarterly board meeting and concentrate on museum issues during that time. Should there be a major issue needing attention at some other time you might gather a quorum but don't count on it. It is not disinterest, just the pressure of time on important people in this busy world of ours. Being aware of this situation, we need to assist the board in carrying out their responsibilities. A well-prepared, well-run quarterly board meeting is a must in this environment. Have a short, tight, focused agenda (short because there will always be issues that arise unexpectedly that generate discussions and take up time you had not planned). Focused because the board needs to be kept abreast of key factors – general operations (visitor count, significant exhibits or collection issues, visitor revenues, special events, major problems, etc.), the financial picture (revenues and expenses compared to budget), marketing strategy, and audit issues. Get key information out to board members prior to the scheduled meetings – agenda, financial report, issue papers. Caution – find the right timing to get best results from this pre-meeting mail-out. You want board members to have had time to peruse the material before the meeting but not to have it overtaken by subsequent events or be received so early as to have been forgotten. Don't ever expect members to bring mailed materials with them to a meeting. Remember they are busy people with crowded agendas. Have a duplicate set at each place at the meeting along with other handouts you plan to use at the meeting. And, speaking of handouts, two rules. First, limit handouts to meaningful, easily understood graph or data sheets that you plan to refer to <u>and</u> cover during the meeting. Second, don't hand out material to be read and digested after the meeting – it is a waste of good paper. On the day of the meeting devote your energies to preparation – room, seating, signage, handouts, audio visual, your notes, food and beverages, greetings etc. Leave an hour free before the meeting to deal with the usual unplanned crisis, last minute changes, comfort issues, board member special requests etc. Once your Chairperson arrives (it is always good to have reminded the chair of the meeting the day prior) he/she will take control, and, with your assistance, run the meeting. Try to start on time even if everyone hasn't shown up – it shows respect for the contribution of valuable time from your board members. This puts the 'discourteous' label on late arriving members, not on the chair or staff for "never starting on time." Also, try very hard to end the meeting on time for the same reason. That way the members can rely on a fixed segment of time for the meeting and are much more likely to attend. It may be helpful to provide an annotated agenda or script to your chair. This expanded agenda can include prompts to give kudos, thank individuals, recognize new members, inject the personal touch, call on committee chairs by name (particularly if you have a large board and substitute or stand-in chairs), include announcements etc.

One way to keep board meetings focused and time sensitive is to be sure the board is informed about significant issues on an on-going basis. Periodic updates using a short "latest news" approach can help keep them up to date on museum happenings, continue to feel a sense of involvement without additional time consuming meetings and have them ready for business when they get to the board meeting. A one or two page monthly or 'on demand' summary of highlights should suffice to dispense with routine operational questions and time consuming discussions at the board meeting.

Despite your best efforts, attendance at board meetings can sometimes be a challenge. Board members are busy, involved people with many demands on their time and constraints on their schedules. Schedule you meetings well in advance – preferably for the whole year at your annual meeting – so they can get on everyone's schedule before the schedules are already full. A good follow-on tactic is to schedule the meetings over the lunch period – e.g. 11:30-1:00 – and provide a light sandwich lunch at the meeting. By inviting members to "grab a plate before we get started" you will accomplish two things – help them be able to attend the entire meeting since they can get lunch at the same time, and recognize the importance of their busy schedule with this courteous 'perk.' Don't make it fancy or complicated, just the opportunity to meet and eat at the same time. A nice approach to allow social interaction, and yet assure attention to the agenda, is to have the chair set the tone by arriving at the appointed time (11:30), greeting other arrivals and eating until 11:55 and then calling the meeting to order and beginning the agenda while attendees are finishing their lunch and late arrivals are getting settled. This scheduling allows for the various personal needs for lunch, no lunch, social time, no social time while it gets the meeting started and, if you have planned the agenda well, ended on time.

Another nice touch to help attendance is to provide readily available on site parking – or if that's not possible, valet parking for these meetings. Not to pander or even pamper, but to recognize the importance of the board members attendance despite their many other commitments. The agenda should be well planned – welcome, call to order, approval of last meeting minutes, committee reports (finance, marketing, collections, fundraising, nominations (annual meeting only), directors remarks (you) which include new issues and highlights of operations not already covered by committees, Chairman's remarks and adjournment. Keep it simple and straight forward - there will be plenty of ad hoc and lively discussions based on questions and answers at each agenda item.

The use of committees, their organization and functions and their participation at board meeting is most flexible. Some committees and their composition are mandated by the charter and bylaws of the organization – most usually nominating, finance, marketing, and collections. On the plus side, committees get board members involved as they take on ownership, and it allows you to tap the wealth of talent, knowledge and expertise they bring to the table. On the minus side, committees can result in a tendency to micro manage, get involved in operational matters as opposed to policy matters, and add workload that consumes valuable staff time. The message is – create board committees where necessary and helpful, not just to give everyone something to do or be involved in.

Selecting and nominating committee chairs is an important task not to be left to chance or political favoritism. The finance committee is going to ask tough questions – both of the staff and the board. It is imperative that the chair be a knowledgeable financial person – CPA, auditor, banker etc. – who can separate wheat from chaff in financial reports, understand the issues from a business point of view and then report on the meaning of pertinent financial developments to the board. Someone who is low key, not alarmist and who can allay unfounded fears with logic can be most helpful in preventing rash and impetuous reactions to financial deviations from the norm or variances from budget. Selecting this committee chair wisely can save much lost time and wasted effort.

Likewise the marketing committee chair should be an expert in the field – in this case a cutting edge expert with good connections in the business who can not only bring experts together to help with the museum program, but who has leverage in the industry to generate free or reduced rates for regular and special advertising campaigns. Riding on coattails here can be a significant cost-saver to the museum.

Collections and /or exhibit committee should be chaired (and populated by) board members with great interest and some expertise in your collections and exhibits. Major accessions or de-accessions must be carefully explained to the board and gain their approval. These are policy issues that fall into the board area of fiduciary and public accountability. Some are likely to be controversial and will need explanation to the board, museum supporters, and the public.

In each case the committee should be staffed by the person on your staff having day to day responsibility for that subject – normally yourself for Executive Committee (chaired by the board chair) and nominating committee, comptroller/accountant/financial manager for the finance committee, marketing/PR/Sales person for marketing committee, etc. Staff persons work with their committee chair to schedule meetings (preferably several weeks before each board meeting so as to be able to present a current report at the meeting), make up the agenda, provide necessary materials for review and decision making, prepare minutes and then assist the committee chair with the necessary report at the board meeting. The committee report can be given by either the committee chair, or a committee member the chair designates, with participation by the museum manager staffing the committee as necessary/desired.

Staff participation in board meetings is dependent on chair and board member desires. Active participation with reports given by senior managers (department heads etc.) gives the board face-to-face contact and the opportunity to hear from the hands-on manager. It can also precipitate board members getting involved in operating matters and cause a shift of board focus from policy to detail. Having senior staff sit in the board meeting can help them understand the background of policy decisions, and improve communication of policy matters to staff. But it can also result in some reduction in candor by board members in the board meetings. Bringing in senior staff for specific agenda item discussions when their knowledge and insight will be valuable to the board is a good compromise. Having the senior staff members who staff the standing committees attend to assist the committee chairs is another good compromise. What is needed is a good balance between open communication of information and closed debate of significant issues. There is no single rule. Personalities, relationships, individual traits and characteristics, and the style of both the board chair and the museum director are the determining factors.

Operating

This is the fun part of the job because it is both challenging and rewarding – frustrating and satisfying. If you have done your homework and gotten this far successfully you are ready to open or reopen your doors to the public. You expect they will flock to your fine museum to be wowed, entertained and educated by its contents and messages. Your "Field of Dreams" is complete and ready. But, just because you built (rebuilt) it, will they come? Maybe. For the big museums who have spent hundreds of millions, done massive (and masterful) PR and pre-opening hype, sport a big name or whose subject matter is the hot button of the day, the interest du jour, the sex appeal of the moment, or fills a known community void, the answer is an unqualified 'yes.'

How about for the rest of us? We are "the little guy" who has spent several millions, garnered what little pro bono PR we could, have no big name recognition and our subject matter is traditional museum or niche without necessarily any great sex appeal. Here the answer is an unqualified 'maybe.' Yes, we should get a good opening bounce - new kid on the block, human curiosity, something new, some good pre-opening PR if we did yeoman's work with the press before opening day, a big deal grand opening drawing card or attraction. But how about when the adrenalin of newness wears off? Here the ball lands squarely in your court. Now is when you earn your pay (modest though it may be) and have the opportunity to succeed. Some of the things worth considering for this phase follow.

Communicate clearly and often with your staff. (We will talk about acquiring and organizing later.) If you have the luxury of departments and department heads, meet with them (all together) daily. I recommend a first thing in the morning 5-minute stand up gathering (it should go no longer than 15 minutes) to quickly go over what's happening throughout the museum that day (or what will be happening tomorrow or over the weekend) that involves several departments. Let each attendee have a minute to speak on what he/she is involved in that day, where help is needed, pass reminders of things due or coming up shortly, etc. This helps make everyone aware of what the rest of the team is doing in real time and what is coming roaring down the road for the next few days. It permits on the spot coordination, highlights problem areas and allows instant resolution and decision making where necessary. It also helps eliminate nasty surprises and conflicts (e.g. 2 tour groups arriving simultaneously when your tour handler had only planned on one), keeps staff from being embarrassed by lack of awareness of what other staff are doing, and generally promotes good staff interaction. By meeting early on in the workday it forces people to think through, and therefore be better prepared for, their day. It gives your staff direct access to you for immediate answers and decisions if necessary. Don't allow it to bog down with details or topics not relevant to its purpose. Policy discussions, new ideas etc. have no place here except to plant seeds for a thought provoking, policy discussion, interactive, brainstorming staff meeting on a less frequent basis but for a longer period – say one hour per week.

Meetings can be the bane of your existence – absorbing valuable time (yours <u>and</u> your staff's), interfering with the necessary daily operating routine, causing boredom and dissatisfaction among the staff etc. Properly used, however, they can be helpful, stimulating, problem solving and even therapeutic. The difference lies in how they are planned, how frequently held and how well they are run. Once a week works for many. More than an hour is normally a real downer, except in unusual cases where the topic is so exciting, so stimulating or so dreadful/important that it keeps everyone on the edge of their seats and requires extra time to come to closure. A written agenda is not necessary but some notes or a mental agenda **is** necessary to keep the discussions on track and on the priority issues. An egalitarian, democratic forum is nice but a benevolent dictatorship forum is more efficient, and, if handled with aplomb, can be equally as effective. Just be careful not to let anyone dominate the meeting if you want to get the best ideas on the table and really hear what's going on in the congregation. Also, don't let everything that comes up just dangle on the hook of indecision. Decisions have to be made, and most don't get easier with time. Rarely will you have perfect or complete information. Rarely will you have time to wait until you can get all that information. Decisions generally have to be made under conditions of uncertainty – get as much information as you can in a reasonable time and then make up your mind and make the best decision you can based on the information available to you and on your past experience. There is risk involved, and you get paid to take some risk. Otherwise perhaps you aren't needed. Whatever you do, don't be like the senior manager who upon being asked to provide a response to a controversial request told his staff to respond with this oxymoron: "Don't tell them 'yes' and don't tell them 'no', but don't be "wishy-washy!" Be decisive, be clear and get on with life. If additional facts come to light after a decision has been made, you can usually revisit the issue and adjust as necessary.

In running your periodic big issue meetings try to make it clear to the group that there are two phases to major issue resolution. The first phase is the discussion phase where all participants have an equal voice, no point of view is less important than another, all parties have something to contribute and all opinions are welcome. In this phase you want a full and open discussion in order to gather as many facts and as much information pro and con as possible so as to reduce the uncertainty when you reach phase two. Phase two is decision making. It can be at the meeting or after the meeting. It is the part where the manager, senior official, responsible party, team leader, or boss must make the best decision he/she can based on the information available, the input received and the advice of the staff and/or parties involved. At this point the discussion phase is **over** and all parties have an ethical obligation to accept the decision and implement it – to get on board, understanding that they have had their day in court. Whether in agreement or not, it is time to accept the decision as policy and fully support it. Unless the decision violates a person's moral or ethical principals, the obligation is to implement it. Should it violate moral or ethical principles, the obligation is to so state to the decision maker and resign if necessary.

Meetings are by definition communications – for better or for worse. So make it for better. We began this book with a discussion of communications – reread it if you wish – concluding that communicating is the weak link in our management system even today. Some of our top darlings of the internet era will fail miserably when an economic downturn comes and they are forced to compete in a tougher environment because they don't know how to really communicate internally. Technology is merely the medium. Communication is the human element that is the substance. Poorly managed businesses can survive in the boom time. Well-managed businesses will be the survivors in the bad times.

OK – you are up and running. You are communicating. What is next? Part of your responsibility is for the physical facility and its condition. Sure you have a good facilities engineer (or whatever moniker you use) but what should you be worried about here? Emergencies! Have a plan. Some are required by law, e.g. fire evacuation! Some are required as part of your fiduciary responsibility, e.g. protection of the museum's physical and financial assets. Some are just common sense – first aid, safety etc. There are lots of ways to address these necessary plans. A series of instructions, a separate "Emergency Plan" publication, posted notices, etc., depending on your style and the precedents set before your arrival. Bottom line – have at least minimal formal plans in place. You probably will have to write them yourself. Help is available.

Other museums (large) are usually happy to give you copies of theirs as a guide. The American Association of Museums can provide good information (I strongly recommend membership even though it consumes some precious dollars), and there are safety-training companies that will come in and set up things for you for a fee. Take your pick, but don't overlook this necessary part of your job. After a theft, fire or major accident is NOT the time to write your plan.

Plans are in place. Now what? Time to be sure you know where everything is, how to get to it and what is going on around you. Your management style will dictate how you do this best. Putting out memos, holding meetings, periodic visits to staff, walking around, etc. Remember to stay out of the "in box – out box, telephone, e-mail" traps. Some things that may be helpful:

- Walk around. It shows your interest, makes you readily accessible to communicate, reveals trouble spots, keeps you knowledgeable on the operations, and gives you a valuable information background from which to make decisions. It also keeps the operation on its toes. (A former "walk-around boss" commented "Nothing stirs the adrenaline flow in the workers veins like the sound of the boss's footsteps.")
- Know every job. Not to the degree that you can do it with ease and expertise, but understand it and be able to pitch in in an emergency. Don't demand of others what you would not do or have not done yourself.
- Be able to get into any space in the museum or that is part of your operation. Insist on a key to every locked area. Go into each occasionally to see what is there and what it looks like. You don't want to be dependent on someone _else_ for access – you never know whether they will be around or available when _you_ need access. If you are there and there is an emergency, you don't want to be helpless re:

access (and look and feel stupid). Know every space and what its purpose and use is. It will help you understand your environment, therefore your job. It will also help you in making decisions – especially space- and storage-related decisions.
- Occasionally poke around at odd times – unusual days, unusual hours. See what goes on when you are not normally around – very early in the morning, late at night, or weekends. It will be preventive of potential mischief, healthy for your staff, give you a much better insight into the totality of your operations and enlighten you about something you might not otherwise understand. It also can give you some quiet, confidential time, and you can work without interference. Try it, you might like it. Some people have even found it so refreshing they change their normal work schedule permanently.
- Intervene when and where necessary. Your staff may be very good. But even the best people have momentary lapses or begin to take things for granted when they are comfortable with them. "Familiarity breeds contempt" may be too strong a statement here, but constant routines can and do cause complacency. Don't let it be beneath your dignity to check thermostats, security, customer/staff interactions, tour guide patter, volume of display sound, operation of interactive displays, signage, lighting, telephone answering manners, etc. Look at the place "for the first time" on a regular basis lest you too become complacent and overlook some small or perhaps even glaring deficiency that can be easily fixed and produce positive, bottom line results.
- Have an open door policy, even if it is restricted to a certain number of hours per day or means an occasional closed door to permit progress on a priority task. In the museum world an open door encourages creativity and open dialogue. Not

everyone thinks or works the same way. Some people will come to you only when they have a crisis – or only when they have a specific well thought out proposal to go over and need approval. Others need to bounce ideas off the boss before they feel comfortable starting down a given path. They need some stimulation to have an idea (or ideas) take shape and rely on you to help get them started. If they have to wait for an appointment or a specific window of time to get to you, their idea and enthusiasm may well be lost as they move to their next crisis, problem, issue or interruption. So be interruptible - plan on it, plan around it, figure it into your days plans and then it will not surprise or frustrate you. It will also pay handsome dividends in helping to focus your staff, helping shape new (hopefully good) ideas and improve efficiency or staff by giving them guidance and/or decisions in a timely manner. Yes, it will often be annoying. Yes, it will also be productive in the big picture.

Revenue Generation

Non-government museums are usually private non-profits. This doesn't mean you don't need to generate revenue. In fact, in today's museum world, success will likely be measured by revenue generated. Yes, the exhibits must be up to par, the facility well designed to integrate exhibits, visitor services, ambiance and education. But, to do all these things – be all you can be – requires money. The more money you garner the better these things can become and the better the staff you can acquire with expertise to be all you can be. Likely then, the trustees will look to you to generate revenue.

Sources are many and varied depending on the type of museum, location, and the policy guidelines from the board. In general (and generalizations are dangerous) there are four broad categories of revenue used by the American Association of Museums. (AAM): earned income, government grants, private contributions, and investment income.

Each major category is divided into a number of sub-categories, which have varying amounts of relevance to different institutions (you may have some or all, and may even have some that no one else does or admits to). For example:

Government Sources:	Federal, State, Local
Private Sources:	Private/Community Foundations
	Corporate Foundations
	Corporations
	Individuals
Investment Income:	Endowment
Earned Income:	General Admissions
	Special Events
	Membership
	Gift Shop and Publications
	Programs and Education
	Food Service
	Royalties
	Other

You notice I have listed earned income differently. That's because this category will give you some of your most agonizing moments. It is here the 'field of dreams' philosophy comes home to roost. Here is where the founders' expectations come head to head with reality and you can be the hero or the scapegoat.

Surveys in the late 1990's were reasonably consistent in indicating that government sources accounted for approximately 30% of museums income, private sources about 23-24%, earned income about 33-34% and investments about 12%. You note that *earned* income is the largest percentage of total representing fully 1/3 of all income. For the small or medium size museum, earned income takes on even more significance, because use or hiring of professional grant request writers or fund-raisers is often not possible with small budgets.

Let's take a brief look at the other categories before we examine earned income.

Grants. There are numerous grants available from government sources for various, often unexplainable and nefarious purposes for every imaginable endeavor from studying the sex life of the tsetse fly to the cause de jour. Surveys reveal local governments as the major source followed by state and finally federal (in contrast to what I guessed in my ignorance). Draw your own conclusions – mine is that local governments often recognize the economic, educational, and cultural value of having museums in their own backyards and believe they deserve public support. For you or your grant request writer (should you be so fortunate to have a fund development staff member) there are publications listing the grants available and giving the criteria for those grants plus lots of advice books on 'how-to.' A check with your contemporaries, the local library, local community foundation, or museum associations will put you on the right track to get started.

Private contributions. Fund development is an art (or science) unto itself. Some experience is necessary here or the road will be long and rocky to achieve even a modicum of success. You probably cannot do it all by yourself unless you are deeply involved in your community personally and know the territory. Otherwise it is best to work with your board to develop the strategy and tactics for fundraising. The board was picked because of their interest in the museum and their status in the community. Hopefully at least one of the members has been involved in philanthropic activity and can provide both guidance and personal support. If you can afford it, it is good to have a staff member devoted to the legwork of fundraising – write materials, work up the plan, work with you and the board in developing the follow-up process, etc. The bottom line here is the absolute necessity *to assure that a process is in place* – strategy, tactics, plan, staff and other resources fully committed to this effort. Remember that some 25% of your funding will probably have to come from this source, AND, 100% of your endowment (which we will address shortly) comes from this source. Fundraising from private sources is critical to both your short-term and long-term survival as an institution. It requires expertise and deserves your attention to keep it on track. It is highly competitive (just look at the number of fund solicitations in your daily mail at home) and a continually changing environment. You need good, solid, expert help and it can be difficult to find. But, it must be done because most museums cannot generate enough earned income to keep the doors open. It is best to discuss the issue with the board chairman before taking the job. What are they doing for private fundraising at present? How successful has it been? Is there a plan or just a 'hit or miss' effort? What percent of the revenue stream does it account for? Is there some expertise on the board and/or on the staff? Can the effort be sustained? Don't take the job without good solid answers to these questions or you may find yourself out on the point doing it all by yourself.

  Investment income. Surveys also show approximately 12% of museum income, on average, comes from investments. It is obvious that assets are necessary to invest to generate this income. Your fundraising efforts must not only generate the revenues you need for operations each year, but also, <u>at some point in time, must provide the major capital needed for your investment portfolio</u> – large cash donations for the endowment fund, revenue generating real estate, stocks, bonds etc. These can come from a major capital campaign or several good patrons who have been very generous and want to assure the museum's survival into perpetuity. The board bears the major responsibility for raising/creating a good endowment – its importance to you is being able to count on a base level of funding each year from its earnings. But even with a good endowment the annual income it throws off for operations is no sure thing. A good deal depends on the investment strategy of the board and such uncertainties as the performance of the stock market, bond market, real estate market and your investment portfolio managers acumen over both the short- and long-term. Small museums seldom have the luxury of being able to retain an investment counselor or portfolio manager. Often the board will task the finance committee or treasurer to look after the investment portfolio. The board may (or may not) establish investment parameters to assure sound management of the endowment. Since it is in essence your "seed corn," be sure someone responsible and financially astute is guarding its integrity.

Finally we get to the 'piece de la resistance' – earned income. This is your sandbox. Lots of people will want to play in your sandbox, but ultimately you will be the one to sweat out the budget each year. You will be challenged – explicitly or implicitly – to build a castle in your sandbox. The mix of tools you have to work with varies based on location, physical configuration, demographics, the economy and your competition. Judging from past surveys, you will probably need to generate sufficient funds to cover about one-third of your budget expenses (presuming your grant, contributions and investment income are reasonably close to the norm). You can be innovative or conservative, try new things or follow the crowd, but, in any case, you will have to work hard to assure success. While it is fun to work on the exhibits, history, organization and management, the essence of your job lies in generating the necessary earned income to stay in business, improve the exhibits and carry out your museum's mission – meet the goals and objectives. Here are some of the more productive elements of earned income to consider.

Nearly universally today's museums like to attract visitors – the more the better. In this endeavor you compete for people's leisure time against every other form of leisure activity in your area – sports, TV, outdoor activities, theme parks, movies, shopping malls, recreation centers, opera, symphony, and other museums within easy driving distance. If you charge an admission fee (most, but not all, museums do) then you compete not only for peoples time, but also for their money.

How to do it? There is no magic formula to fit all museums. For some it is the sheer magnitude of their presentation – the "gee-whiz" or "wow" factor of the museum itself. Usually these are new big museums like the Getty, the Tech, Boeing, etc. Others depend heavily on a cohesive, well-planned, time-phased marketing plan to gain brand name recognition and generate interest so you will come to mind when they say to themselves "What shall we do today? Or this weekend?" Intriguing and well-advertised exhibits – traveling, rotating, temporary, etc. – can be a dominant factor. I recall the Bishop Museum, Hawaii's State Museum of Culture and History, bringing in a traveling exhibit on dinosaurs to Hawaii and the stir it caused, bringing thousands of new visitors to the museum.

Then there are promotions – special days, special events (e.g. the Hiller Aviation Museum/Radio Disney "Happy Noon Year" celebration at noon on December 31 for the younger set and their parents) – that drew a capacity crowd on what otherwise would have been a slow museum day. These can generate lots of free publicity, build excitement, and feature special events ranging from typical lecture series forums to celebrity cameos.

Special occasions – free days, anniversary of opening, holiday celebrations (Santa Claus, Easter egg hunt, etc.) are always attractions if well promoted. Previews, meet the artist, book signings, private showings, auctions, fundraisers and many more can be cleverly crafted to both gain attention and bring visitors to you. And there can always be special programs for select audiences – school children, scouts, the underprivileged, seniors, senior centers, convention goers, convention spouse tours, etc. The number of ideas here is only limited by your imagination and that of your staff.

What happens when you've tried them all and your admissions have leveled off below the 'field of dreams' numbers or below the board's expectations? Or more importantly below your budget and its expected revenue from visitor fees? What then?

First and foremost remember that admissions are not the only game in town when it comes to earned income. Don't give up on it – there are always new good ideas to reach out and attract visitors. So don't panic just yet. Before you start beating on your marketing person, step back and see what else is available to you to help keep the doors open, the lights and air-conditioning on, meet the payroll and guarantee survival into (hopefully) perpetuity.

A hot button for museums in a robust economy can be unique, exciting venues for private, company or organization events. An IPO announcement, a stockholders meeting, a company celebration, a new rich 40th birthday party, a major division of a large company with a sales, new product or attitude adjustment gathering, and many more like them present golden opportunities for medium sized museums to generate earned income through rental of museum facilities ranging from the main gallery or galleries to special meeting rooms and from full-blown mega parties to small intimate affairs. And you don't need a full blown catering capability. The museum can be nothing more then a "bare boat charter" – you sell (rent-out) the space and the renting party arranges all the rest – caterer, music and sound system, decorations, special lightening, tables and chairs from a rental company, etc. While this can be a grand revenue source for a museum, there are some alligators out there that need to be handled first.

Several key elements are necessary in a successful facilities rental program. Before you begin you must have a good, clear, straight-forward, and very tight contract for use of your facilities that covers all the bases, including pricing, overtime charges, security, cleaning charges, restrictions, alcohol, release of liability deposits (refundable and non-refundable), parking, set-up times and restrictions, fire regulations, rental companies parameters, caterer parameters, decorations and their restrictions, audio visual, tenting (if allowed), insurance, non-smoking, tour guides (if provided) and other considerations peculiar to your facility. Floor layout and map to the facility are helpful inclusions. You will also need a good (preferably a great) event coordinator – someone on your staff who has a full-time responsibility to solicit, book, contract for and personally oversee each and every event facility rental– to facilitate, coordinate and then control all elements from setup to cleanup and lockup. Don't underestimate the importance of this position. He/she is the key element in generating the *net* revenue flow to the museum.

Without very close scrutiny the program can be a great success for the party giver but a cash flow loss to you. Make certain you know the NET profit from this effort – the gross might be great but it is the NET to you that counts. Remember you must cover the incremental utilities (after all the events aren't going to use your facility in the dark or cold or heat), cleaning, cost of security, <u>wear and tear</u> on the facilities, your staff (wages plus fringes) etc. If you decide to go with full service where you provide tables, chairs, audio/visual, etc., a reserve fund for replacement costs will also need to be included as those things will wear out very quickly and need to be replaced. More than one museum has discovered that if not closely monitored their great gross from events (looks good on income side) became a net-loss after considering both direct and indirect costs (looks bad on expenses side if you break it out) and you have lots of work and hassle so <u>others</u> can make money and have fun at your special events and you help pay for their fun! Not a good idea!! A good, tough, strict, practical and knowledgeable special events/facilities rental coordinator can prevent this from happening. But he/she will need **your** backing to hold the line both with the rest of your staff (who may have a tendency to want to give away the store to enhance their particular programs or interests) and with the clients and service personnel (caterers, electrical, audio visual, rental equipment, decorators etc.) who will run all over your rules and restrictions if allowed to do so. Drinking, dining, dancing and smoozing in the ambiance of your unique facility, exhibits, displays, art and artifacts can be a memorable occasion for the guests – one that can be revenue enhancing to you, good word of mouth publicity for your venue and also bring people back. Used properly, facility rental is a winner all around.

Then there is your gift shop. Chances are your visitor would be interested in a little souvenir or memento of the visit or may even have an avocation that matches with your theme and is looking for something to add to a collection, or library, or some object related to your mutual interest. What better place to find it than at your museum. Done properly it is a win-win – your visitor finds what he/she wants in an atmosphere of mutual interest, and you make a small profit that goes to your bottom line. Simple? Not really. The missing ingredient is "retailing". I am not even remotely an expert and chances are you are not either. So we need to get an expert, set some realistic parameters such as amount we can afford to invest in and tie up in inventory, expected turnover rate of inventory, margins, range of merchandise, sales per visitor targets, amount of space/square feet available, etc., and then turn him/her loose while keeping a sharp eye on the parameters set. The right merchandise, aimed at the right crowd, in the right location, and in the right market can sizzle. While amount of space devoted to the gift shop is a factor, it may not be the critical factor. A <u>very</u> small retail gift shop at the Waikiki Aquarium in Honolulu with a limited variety of high tourist appeal items did a land office business eclipsing many larger local rivals in sales/visitor, total sales and net profit. It was in the right location (near the entrance/exit, in plain view), well lighted, well staffed, attractive, with popular items of the time, nice price points and with very courteous staff. The pull to the visitor was irresistible – a memento of the island, of the sea, of the aquarium – a gift for relatives back home from 'paradise', - a fun toy, game or clothing item for the kids. Well done, successful – in a cubbyhole for space. Or an art museum with a great selection of 'artsy', intelligent, challenging upscale items – interesting gifts, books for collectors and unique jewelry. Or the medium sized aviation museum with a hugh retail space boasting the best selection of aviation books on the west coast and covering every conceivable aviation item from trinkets to jewelry to models, to make your own models, to flight jackets, kites etc. etc. Again – no magic cook book recipe for all – just attention to business – your business and your environment. Know your audience (customers) and carry what they want or what you know they will buy if they see it. Have something for everyone – everyone who is most likely to visit your museum and be exposed to your gift shop. A well-planned, well-executed gift shop should gross at least 50% as much as your admission income and could equal or exceed it. *Net* profit should be targeted to be at least 40% of gross sales.

Membership. A marginally successful membership program works off a "support your museum" theme. A more successful one appeals to a persons desire to participate, be among an elite group and gain some personal benefit and *stature* from belonging. Designed properly it can be rewarding for members to join and rewarding for your bottom line. Such a program requires exemplary attention to detail (who among us wants to have our name misspelled when we donate or contribute money), some caste (tiered) system of membership to appeal to all levels and abilities to participate, and then some perks – not necessarily trinkets or giveaways like the junk mail solicitations – but some genuine prerogatives and ego satisfiers like invitations to members-only pre-opening new exhibit previews, opportunities to meet the artist or author or designer in an intimate setting, public recognition in your venue (plaque on the "Donor Wall" with name engraved, sponsorship acknowledgment etc.). Such a program also requires prompt acknowledgment of membership, prompt follow-up on member requests, *personal* follow-up on tardy renewals and a meticulously kept database.

Food service. While food service can be an earned income source, it is more valuable as a service to the visitors – making a visit to your museum a fun, comfortable, lingering, family experience. It provides a respite, and generally enhances the visitors' impression and experience. Just like a wafting smell of home-baked cookies can help sell houses, so a pleasant, inviting, clean, aromatic food service can leave a lasting sensual impression on your visitors. If it also adds to the bottom-line directly, so much the better.

These then are some of the earned revenue possibilities. There may be others depending on the particular locale, museum, venue and time. Be alert for business opportunities but be wary of the hucksters who will try to convince you that their wares will eliminate all your worries. There is no free lunch. If some new money making idea seems too good to be true, it probably is. Remember the goal is to minimize the reliance on earned revenue so as to reduce the risk to the museum during economic slowdowns, increases in competition, changes in people's tastes for leisure time activities and the other vagaries of the market place. A good healthy, well-managed endowment fund can be a great shield and buffer to the unexpected, unpredictable, or even catastrophic exogenous variables.

Staffing

There is no magic here. Likewise there is no "model" structure. The challenge is to have an organization that gets everything done that needs to be done and at the same time works efficiently. The key parameters are just that simple – effectiveness and efficiency. If the group is effective but not efficient, then the bloat is in expenses and it immediately is reflected at the bottom line. If the group is efficient but not effective, then the hurt is in delivering of programs and services, reputation and popularity, and while the effect is delayed in getting to the bottom line, it will get there.

We have previously discussed the various characteristics of staff and the distinct importance of the hiring and management of people. But the question here is not the people but the structure. What do you need in the way of expertise and how do the parts of the resulting puzzle fit together to give a comprehensible whole – an organization (of people) capable of efficiently facilitating the achievement of your museum objectives – education, entertainment, satisfaction, revenue and delivery of your 'goods' and services.

Lets go back to the beginning. What are the functional needs of a self-sufficient medium sized museum? The basics are straightforward. A modern museum is a business; what functions are necessary to run a business? A business operates, sells and must be funded and kept up. That's an operations manager, a marketing (and public relations and community relations and promotions) director, a fundraiser and a facilities maintenance person. There is the heart, soul and body of the organization. It needs a head, so you are elected as curator, or director, or CEO and/or maybe COO, dependent on your board.

That's the nucleus: director, operations, marketing, fundraising and maintenance. Of course, it is bare bones. There are many more tasks and functions needing attention. We may or may not have the luxury of being able to provide separate people for each. But we want to at least know what those other areas are. Here are some of the most common:

Finance:	accounting, accounts payable, contracts, insurance, leases, audit, payroll, supplies
Administration:	human resources, budget, clerical, receptionist, training, office equipment, postal, computer systems
Museum:	archives, collections management, exhibits, library, historian, registrar
Events:	school groups, tours, facilities rentals, special events
Education:	programs, curriculum, forums, exchanges
Volunteers:	acquisition and training for docents, tour guides, and restoration shop workers
Restoration:	exhibits, artifacts restoration

And your core:

Operations:	admissions (ticket sales), retail sales (gift shop and food service), concessions, vending
Marketing:	advertising, sales, public relations, promotions, community relations
Maintenance:	facilities, utilities, vehicles, grounds, safety, security
Fundraising:	grant writing, fund solicitation, membership

Mix and match is the order of the day here depending on the variables of each situation. Multi-tasking is normal for smaller museums. But almost all of the functions are required no matter what the size of the museum. So besides multi-tasking, it is not unusual to contract out some functions (payroll is a good example) particularly where the function requires a particular skill or expertise that is a scarce or expensive commodity and/or the need is only periodic, sporadic or much less than deserves a full time staff member. Other functions can be handled by part time staff where the quality expertise is available and the need or workload is less than full time. In fact, sometimes great expertise can be acquired for a reasonable cost on a part time basis from the retired community. Screen your volunteer pool – usually a rich potpourri of experience and expertise – when you have an intermittent, short term or part time functional need. You'll be surprised at what turns up!

Now – how do you organize this broad spectrum of talent so as to get an effective, efficient, functioning staff? With some difficulty! There are many models regarding organization (or lack there of) and the old saying "If you don't like weather, just wait and it will change" applies. Every school of management, every management book writer, every guru of business, has the "latest" hot theory of organizing work. From the ultra conservative line and staff wiring diagram with its hierarchy of authority and delineation of responsibility, to the ultra liberal Silicon Valley 'brainstorm together' without structure approach, the variations on the theme are many. Bottom line – it has to work for your museum and with your people. Best thing here is to fit the organization to your needs and around the expertise and personalities of the people you have. Then make certain you communicate to all concerned what the assignment of responsibilities and authority is or is not. If you have the courage and confidence, you might also explain the rational to all concerned. This can be risky in terms of bruising some egos and causing some division within the group, but it will clearly delineate sandbox boundaries where necessary and set in motion the process of performance evaluations against expectations. The less formal the arrangement, the more flexibility available to manage and address new workload and unplanned responsibilities. The more formal the arrangement, the less confusion as to who is supposed to be doing what. Whatever is done in this organizational effort, be sure *you* know what you expect from each member of the group.

A Final Word

As the managing director, executive director, chief executive, or chief operating officer, you are responsible for the health and well being of the museum. It can be a fun adventure or a mind numbing experience – or a little of each. In the final analysis your ability to work with people, your management skills and to a lesser extent your technical knowledge of museum operations, will influence the outcome. Set realistic goals and objectives with your board chair, build a competent and cohesive team, think outside of the box, and mind the store for the best chance of success. Success is never guaranteed, and is measured by different yardsticks in different circumstances. There are very many exogenous variables in the museum success equation. These you have no control over and can only react to. Luck is a factor – but as the old saying goes – "the harder I work, the luckier I get". Good luck!

Chapter X

Mystical Management Made Simple

The gurus of management teach outstanding principles and techniques. Insight from success stories and lessons from experiences abound. Even "how to" books and courses are plentiful. That being so, why aren't we all perfect managers, better leaders, or successful every time?

There are lots of reasons because there are lots of variables. And as the sage once said, "the only thing that stays constant is change." The environment around us is in a constant state of change. What once was a successful technique or principle becomes outmoded. Witness the internet technology impact on our economic models, market forces, and ways of conducting commerce. It is perhaps the single best example of how changes beyond our control impact a manager's daily life, successful techniques and the ground rules for managing. Those who don't recognize the need to change become obsolete like the buggy whip or extinct like the dinosaur. Stock brokerage firms quickly discovered they needed to change, adapt, or be left out as on-line stock trading became a significant player in the market.

In addition to technology driven change affecting management dictates, societal and cultural conditions affect what works in management. It used to be people had a great deal of respect for other people in positions of authority. In that cultural environment the authoritarian style worked very well. Kings, prophets, teachers, etc. could all dictate behavior by virtue of their physical, moral, or educational authority. Today not so. At one time logic, right verses wrong, reason, and rational thought were tools of persuasion that could be counted on to be successful for managers because others listened, understood, and responded rationally. Not necessarily so today.

Moral persuasion also once worked as a useful tool of managers. The 'common good' or needs of society, or even 'good of country' logic could be successfully applied. But, with the prevalence of the "me first" attitude in society today, this is no longer a certain road to management success. I distinctly recall being sternly lectured by a member of congress during the recess of a congressional budget hearing at which I had taken an opportunity to invoke the "national interest and well being of our citizens" argument in support of an obvious 'motherhood and apple pie' issue in a budget request. His pointedly delivered warning to me went something like this "… I don't ever want to hear you invoke the national interest in front of me again. The national interest is about number six on my list of priorities. My first priority is getting reelected, second is taking care of my constituents, third is what is good for my state, fourth is what is good for my party, fifth is what is best for this body (congress) and then, and only then am I concerned with the national interest!…". Needless to say I was left speechless! But it taught me an important lesson: self-interest can, and often does outweigh all else in our society. It is a weakness of the human condition. As managers we need to understand the human condition with all of its weaknesses and strengths, all of its nobleness' and its warts and hairs. And then manage accordingly.

Also, people's needs change. Maslov's hierarchy of needs still applies at the base levels – food, shelter, etc. – but depending on ones place in today's society and economy, the higher level needs may change. Acceptance, recognition, feeling of productivity, stature, ego satisfaction, self-worth and self-esteem, confidence, visibility, independence, decision making authority, free time, etc., all become particularly important to comfortable people and therefore are factors to be considered in management decisions. What works with one person won't necessarily produce the best result with another. What is important to one person today may not be his/her priority tomorrow. The variables are infinite. You need to have an equally infinite number of options in your personal "play-book" to deal with them. Not a trivial challenge! But there are some common threads – some themes – that run through all of these variables that make easier the task of satisfying people's various and varying needs as you manage.

In my 'play book' they are not techniques or specific actions but rather philosophies and attitudes that, when overlaid on the day to day management challenges seem to make it easier to pick a course of action or response that has a high probability of successful outcome both in the solving the problem *and* satisfying people's varying needs.

Reviewing the philosophies and attitudes of successful managers can be a useful and even enlightening exercise. It can be equally as instructive to review some unsuccessful attitudes and philosophies! You might look at successful (by your definition) peers, mentors, superiors, community leaders, national leaders, world leaders, or people who are well liked and/or well respected. Compile a list for yourself and then see what fits and works for you. My preferential list would include these:

- Be true to yourself and your core values.
- Be honest and truthful.
- Have integrity.
- Be straightforward but not abrasive.
- Be open and frank.
- Try to always maintain *positive* relationships.
- Always look after your subordinates.
- Try to cooperate with your peers.
- Tell it like it is.
- Accept feedback gracefully.
- Have and use a good sense of humor.
- Set boundaries.
- Always respect human dignity.
- If you must criticize, criticize actions not individuals.
- Don't shoot the messenger.
- Don't overreact.
- Always be open to others' good ideas.
- Try to surround yourself with people who are smarter than you are and listen to them with an open mind.

- Be flexible.
- Work hard but don't make it your life.
- Remember everyone has something to offer.
- Keep an open door.
- Be a good listener.
- Be decisive.
- Stand up and be counted when it counts.
- Don't fall on your sword over trivia.
- Don't burn bridges – you might need them.
- Put policies in writing.
- Communicate, communicate, communicate.
- A generalist knows less and less about more and more, a specialist knows more and more about less and less – decide which you want to be.
- Don't be a fence sitter.
- Know the territory – your job, the plant, the people, the competition, the ground rules.
- Compliment in public; criticize in private.
- Don't let ego overcome good judgment.
- Be cautious but not fearful.
- When making crucial decisions under uncertainty, look at the best case and the worst case outcomes and be sure you can live with the worst case if it happens.
- Appreciate bright people and don't be intimidated by them – only insecure people worry about being pushed out.
- Remember, the higher you climb the more your behind shows.
- Tomorrow you may need help from the 'little person' you help along today.
- Give the responsible party a chance to correct a problem before you go over his/her head to their boss.
- Stand strong for what is right even if it is unpopular.
- Make others feel like they are a worthwhile part of the team.
- Plan twice; execute once.

- Do the right things, and then do these things right.

If you succeed in following most of these you will be a good bet to get through those pearly gates! But, do you need to follow them to succeed? Of course not. There are plenty of success stories by rude, abrasive, dishonest, selfish, demeaning, demanding, pompous managers. Do the above listed philosophies and attitudes guarantee success? No, but they certainly get you into the game. What they will do is give you a good foundation for successful management, focus your energy on issues, allow you to be at peace with yourself, let you enjoy what you do and gain the respect of others. In the final analysis you have to look yourself in the mirror each day and be satisfied in mind and heart with what you see. Worldly success is fleeting – it can't buy health, happiness or peace of mind. Yet, health, happiness, and peace of mind are what make life worth living! Remember life is a journey, not a destination. Try to enjoy the trip!

You and I cannot cure all the ills of the world. But we CAN make a difference by being good managers – good stewards of resources entrusted to us. Work at it, think about it, enjoy it, and you will succeed. Happy managing!